THE HOLY SPIRIT

THE HOLY SPIRIT

THE MISSING INGREDIENT

FREDERICK K. C. PRICE

THE HOLY SPIRIT: THE MISSING INGREDIENT
by Frederick K.C. Price
Published by Creation House
7901 South Vermont Avenue
Los Angeles, California 90044

This book is produced and distributed by Creation House, a Charisma Media Company, www.charismamedia.com.

Unless otherwise noted, all Scripture quotations are from the King James Version of the Bible.

Scripture quotations marked ESV are from the Holy Bible, English Standard Version, copyright © 2001 by Crossway Bibles, a division of Good News Publisher. Used by permission.

Design Director: Justin Evans

Cover design by Justin Evans

Visit the author's website: www.faithdome.org.

Library of Congress Cataloging in Publication Data:
2016938899
International Standard Book Number: 978-1-62998-538-1
E-book International Standard Book Number:
978-1-62998 539 8

While the author has made every effort to provide
accurate telephone numbers and Internet addresses
at the time of publication, neither the publisher nor
the author assumes any responsibility for errors or for
changes that occur after publication.

21 22 23 24 25 — 98765432

CONTENTS

PREFACE

WHEN JESUS CAST the demons out of the Gadarene demoniac and was about to leave that region, the man out of whom the demons had departed desired to go with Him. But Jesus sent him away saying: "Return to thine own House, and shew how great things God hath done unto thee. And he went his way, and published throughout the whole city how great things Jesus had done unto him" (Luke 8:38–40). In other words, what Jesus was saying to this man, in so many words, was, "Go and give your testimony!"

That is what has prompted me, along with the guidance of the Holy Spirit, to tell "how great things the Lord has done for me." So it is scriptural to give one's personal testimony, and that's what this book is all about. I want to share with the household of faith that which I have experienced with the Lord.

The baptism with the Holy Spirit is a very active issue in these times. There is so much unnecessary fear and misunderstanding about it. I want to share my experience that it might be used of the Lord to bring many more of His hungering, thirsting children into that place of full joy and victory. The enemy would have us remain in the dark concerning this great and important issue. But thanks be to God that the entrance of His Word brings light (Ps. 119:130).

If you desire to be used of the Lord in the fullest sense and to come into that place of full joy, victory, and power, this story may help point you in that direction. I, too, for many years sought to serve the Lord with my full being but always found myself limited by something that I could not put my finger on. I thought the problem was external, but in reality the problem was within.

The Lord showed me that in order to serve Him with my full life, I must have power. And He is the only one who can give that power. I always thought that I had all that God had to give when I received Christ as my personal Savior, but I found that that was untrue. When you come right down to it, the only reason I thought that was because that's what everyone said. Many leading Bible authorities had taught that we received the Holy Spirit and all of His gifts at conversion. Well, the Bible teaches differently, and thank God I found it out.

The joy and the victory in prayer and in every other area of Christian life I never knew until I came into the baptism with the Holy Spirit. Believe me when I tell you that it's real. This is my story.

I share it with you in the hope that you, too, may come to know Jesus, not only as Savior and Lord, but also as the Baptizer with the Holy Spirit.

THE MISSING LINK

THERE WAS A nagging sensation within me that something was wrong, something was missing. I knew that there was no power being manifested in my life or, as far as I could see, in the life of the church.

For many months I had been completely dissatisfied with our Wednesday night prayer services. They seemed so empty and formal. There was a lack of conviction, real joy, and victory. Our prayers seemed to be rising no further than the ceiling. There was a dimension of the Christian life and experience that was lacking, but I didn't know what it was.

Every time I read the words of Jesus in John 14:12: "...the works that I do shall he do also; and greater works than these shall he do; because I go unto my Father," it left me longing. I was not witnessing these "greater works" in my own ministry or in the ministry of others that I knew with two exceptions— Kathryn Kuhlman and Oral Roberts.

I had read Kathryn Kuhlman's first book, *I Believe in Miracles*,[1] and it stirred my soul. This was the missing dimension—the demonstration of the power of the Spirit of God. Every time I read the Gospels and the Book of Acts, I was impressed with the demonstrations of power that were manifested throughout—signs, miracles, and healings.

2

SEEK AND YE SHALL FIND

O N DECEMBER 25, 1969, my wife, Betty, the
kids and I spent the day with Betty's Aunt
Tena. We had turkey and all the trim-
mings. Tena wanted us to celebrate Christ's birthday
together. I was determined just to sit around and
relax the whole day. And that's exactly what I did.
While lounging in the living room, my eyes fell on
a book lying on a table. The picture on the front
caught my attention—it was Kathryn Kuhlman.
When I read the title, *God Can Do It* Again,[1] I said
to myself, "This must be more about miracles that
God is performing through her ministry."

I picked up the book and headed for the den. I
found a comfortable chair and sat down to read. I
couldn't put the book down. As I read each account,
I felt a strange sensation come over me. I began to
cry tears of joy as I read story after story of how the
power of God was healing and changing lives today,
in our time. I read every chapter in tears—tears of

3

joy and tears of revelation and discovery. I realized that this was what I was longing for—the manifestation of the power of God, the same kind of power that was evidenced in the life and ministry of Jesus Himself. After reading and discovering that all these miracles were the result of the operation of the Holy Spirit, I was determined to seek the appropriation of the operation of the Holy Spirit in my own life and ministry.

I knew that Kathryn Kuhlman came to the Shrine Auditorium in Los Angeles once a month. I knew also from reading her books that if you wanted a seat you had to arrive early on that Sunday morning and stand in line until the doors opened. Even then, there was no guarantee that you would get a seat. I desired very much to go to one of those services to observe firsthand what was happening.

Being a pastor and having the responsibility of preaching every Sunday, I doubted whether I would have the opportunity to go to one of the services. There was no way that I could justify leaving my own congregation to go somewhere else. I had just about given up hope of ever going when I discovered that our own choir director was singing with the Kathryn Kuhlman choir that sang at the services every month. She told me that she could get me in on her pass, so I could leave my church and arrive at the Shrine just in time for the service. She also said that it would be possible for me to sit on the platform. Well, that was more than I ever dared to hope for.

IN HIS PRESENCE

THE DAY WAS January 18, 1970; and it was with great expectation that I walked across the platform and took my seat on that Sunday evening. As the choir began to sing, electricity shot up and down my spine. Finally, the choir began to sing "He Touched Me," and Miss Kuhlman walked on stage. It was like a signal and everyone stood up and began applauding and joining in with the choir singing "He Touched Me," "He's the Savior of My Soul," and finally, "How Great Thou Art."

My joy overflowed. Tears were streaming down my face. I knew that I was in the presence of the Almighty. The service was fantastic. People from all over the great auditorium were coming forward claiming to have been healed of all sorts of ailments—from deafness to cancer. Here were miracles happening right before my very eyes! I imagine I felt like those people felt in the city of Jerusalem during the days of the earthly ministry of Christ: here was power, here were the greater works that Jesus had referred to so many centuries before.

I knew in that moment that this was the answer. Miss Kuhlman was saying that all these miracles were the direct result of the manifestation of the power of the Holy Spirit. Not only that, but she further stated that she felt these signs, wonders, and miracles should be happening in every church across the world. I knew in my heart that she was right.

The one thing that day that really turned me on was Miss Kuhlman's announcement about the subject on which she planned to preach on her return to the Shrine on February 15, 1970. Can you guess what it was? *The Holy Spirit!* I almost fell off my chair! The conviction came to me immediately that I was on the right track. I left the Shrine that day determined to seek the power of the Holy Spirit.

THE WORD OF THE LORD

ONE DAY SHORTLY thereafter, it was impressed upon me to read the entire Book of Acts, paying special attention to every reference made concerning the activities of the Holy Spirit. It was Monday, my day off; and I drove down to the beach at Santa Monica to be alone. I parked as close as I could to the ocean and opened my Bible to the Book of Acts. As I read, I noticed that every time the Holy Spirit manifested Himself, something happened—something definite and spectacular happened.

The apostles preached and witnessed to the reality of Christ with a power that could not be withstood. Not only that, but in every case where someone received the Holy Spirit or the fullness of the Spirit, something happened. There was a manifestation that indicated to the person receiving the Holy Spirit and to those standing by that something most definite had occurred.

In many references, the scriptures plainly stated that those who received the Holy Spirit spoke in "unknown tongues" immediately. This was the evidence. It was truly amazing. I saw this and yet I didn't see it. I saw it, but I didn't understand it. How blind we can be sometimes! I had been taught that everyone who received Christ as their personal Savior automatically received the Holy Spirit at the same time. Therefore, every time I read these passages in Acts about "unknown tongues" being related to the initial receiving of the Holy Spirit, my mind drew a blank.

Many times we Christians miss the blessings the Lord has for us because of our prejudiced minds. Many times we believe what men say without ever really consulting the Word of God. I later learned that what really happens is the Holy Spirit receives us at the time of conversion and baptizes us into the body of Christ. We then become members of His body and that makes us one with Him.

That's one thing; but we still need power to function in the body, and that's where the baptism with the Holy Spirit comes in. Remember, in the first chapter of Acts, Jesus was talking to His disciples and He said: "But ye shall receive power, after that the Holy Ghost is come upon you" (Acts 1:8).

Surely if they who walked and talked with Jesus

needed this power in operation in their lives, how much more do we today need it.

A FRIEND SPEAKS

URING THE WEEK of February 8, 1970, I received a phone call from a friend of mine, Jack Goffigon—a chaplain with the Central Jail in downtown Los Angeles. He invited me to have lunch with him the following week. In the meantime, Miss Kuhlman was coming back to the Shrine on the 15th. Remember, she was supposed to speak on the subject of the baptism with the Holy Spirit. Since her meeting in January, Miss Kuhlman had been to Vietnam and back. So, on the 15th, instead of preaching about the Holy Spirit, she talked about her trip to Vietnam. As you can well imagine, I was disappointed beyond description.

Jack and I met for lunch on Thursday, February 19, 1970. Out of the clear blue, during our conversation over lunch, he began to relate an experience he had had several years before. He said that his life and ministry had been so empty, so void of power. But one day at a meeting he attended with several other ministers, he was introduced to the subject of the baptism with the Holy Spirit. When the meeting was over and the men were standing around in groups of two and three, someone asked him if he was interested in receiving the gift of the Holy Spirit. He said he was.

The man told him that he was going to lay hands on him and pray as the apostles had done in the first century. Jack said he had no idea what to expect. He was told to ask the Lord to baptize him with the Holy Spirit. He did this and then it happened, just like on the day of Pentecost: he opened his mouth and began speaking in "unknown tongues." He told me that he was both amazed and thrilled. Since that day, his joy has been full.

I was fascinated. I related to him how I was feeling and what I was experiencing. It sounded just like his experience prior to receiving the gift of the Holy Spirit. As we parted that day, he said that he had some books that he thought I would be interested in that might be helpful in resolving my problem. They were *Face Up with a Miracle* by Don Basham,[1] *They Speak with Other Tongues* by John Sherrill,[2] and *This Awakening Generation* by John H. Osteen.[3]

LIGHT AND DARKNESS

As I look back on that time, I stand in awe at the realization that God uses human instruments to bring a hungering, seeking child of His to that place of joy and fulfillment. I left Jack and headed for the office determined to read all three of the books—not knowing what to expect—but hoping to find my answer.

I read *Face Up with a Miracle* first and was immediately struck with the conviction that this was it. After reading the very first chapter, I knew without a doubt that God was leading me. As I read Basham's account of his hunger and thirst after that missing dimension in his own life, I thought for a moment that I was reading my own story.

I finished *Face Up with a Miracle* and read the other two books with the deepening conviction that I was about to reach the end of my quest. When I finished the last book, I knew this was it: the baptism with the Holy Spirit and the evidence of speaking with other tongues was what I was looking for. This was the doorway into that supernatural realm of the manifestation of the power of God.

In order to do the works and "greater works" that Jesus did, we must have the same enabling power that He had. And thank God that power is available to us today. Looking back over His life, it is strikingly evident that Jesus did not set about to do any ministry work until He had been anointed with the Holy Spirit at John's baptism (Matt. 3:13–17). That is why He could do the works that He did—because the Spirit of the Lord was upon Him. He needed to be filled with the Spirit of God. I, too, needed this enabling power in order to be an effective witness for Jesus. That was the missing ingredient: spiritual power!

This somewhat confused me at first because, as I said earlier, I had been taught that every believer received the Holy Spirit the moment he believed and received Christ. But what I discovered after reading these books and checking the scriptures again was that in reality the Holy Spirit receives us into the body of Christ and forms Christ within us. He takes up His residence within us and a well of water begins to bubble up into everlasting life within our lives. In other words, the Spirit baptizes us into the body of Christ. But in order to really live the overcoming, joyous, and victorious life in Christ, we must go one step further and allow Jesus Himself to baptize us with the Holy Spirit. Then and only then does the well that was established at conversion burst forth and become rivers of living water. That is when the power comes, and that was what was missing in my life and ministry. I saw this and was thrilled; thrilled because this power was mine to have and was available to me at that very moment.

In *Face Up with A Miracle*, it is stated that anyone can receive the Holy Spirit in the privacy of his own room. All that is necessary is to ask Jesus, by faith, to baptize you; then open your mouth and speak in other tongues as the Spirit gives utterance.[1]

Well, it was late by then; but I was determined to put into execution what I had discovered. However, many times we are not aware of the hang-ups that reside within us. I knew so well and had even taught and preached on the fact that we cannot rely on feelings or emotions when seeking things of God. I didn't realize how hung up I was with regard to feelings until that moment.

I followed the instructions as they were written and nothing happened. Let me say it again: nothing happened! I was crushed beyond measure. Tears streamed down my face as I pleaded with God for the Holy Spirit; but nothing happened, nothing came. I was completely demoralized. With tears in my eyes I headed home. My wife knew that something was wrong when I came in looking utterly dejected. I told her what I had discovered in the books and my effort to receive the Holy Spirit—and how miserably I had failed.

7

HOPE ARISES

THE SUN ROSE on Friday, February 20, 1970; but it was a gloomy day for me. I was disgusted and frustrated as I drove to the church. Arriving at the office I decided to go over the books again to see if I had missed anything or misread some of the instructions. After several hours, the thought occurred to me that I might need the help of someone who had already received the Holy Spirit. I remembered reading in John Sherrill's book about a Harald Bredesen who had received the gift of the Holy Spirit.

I leafed through the book and found the reference I was looking for. But, Harald Bredesen was in New York and that was a long way from Los Angeles. At this point I was becoming very agitated and had just about decided to use my TWA credit card—you guessed it—to fly to New York and find Harald Bredesen.

While this thought was turning over in my mind,

the name Dennis Bennett caught my eye. Reading along, I discovered, to my happy surprise, that he pastored a church nearer to me on the West Coast—Seattle, Washington, to be exact. I thought, "This is right in my own backyard!" I noticed in John Sherrill's account that Father Bennett had a service every Friday night known as an "information service" but designed especially for those seeking the Holy Spirit. This was it! Just what I was looking for, and this was Friday!

I wondered what time the service was held, so I decided before making a reservation on a flight to Seattle that I would call and find out the time. When I reached the church secretary she told me the time of the service and then added, "But I'm sorry, Father Bennett is out of town today." I don't have to tell you what happened inside me, do I? I will leave that to your imagination.

I told her I was calling from Los Angeles and greatly desired to talk with Father Bennett. Then she made a statement that again fired my hopes. Father Bennett was speaking in the Los Angeles area. Choking back the excitement in my voice, I asked her if she knew his itinerary. She told me to hold on while she checked. Waves of excitement were rolling over me as I waited.

With a note of regret, she informed me that she could not find it anywhere; but she could give me the name and number of the people with whom he was staying nearby in the San Fernando Valley. That was good enough for me. Thanking her, I hung up and dialed the number in the Valley. No answer! I tried again; still no answer. I called that number most of the day and never reached anyone. Now frantic, I called Seattle again hoping that by now the secretary had found the list of his speaking engagements. She was sorry, but she hadn't.

Completely shattered, I asked if she knew of anyone, *anyone at all*, in the Los Angeles area who could help me in my quest. She thought for a moment and said there was one person she was sure could help me. The fires of hope began to burn within me again. His name was Larry Christenson and he pastored a Lutheran church in San Pedro. That was all she knew. I told her "Thank you, I will find him." I was determined to go over San Pedro with a fine-tooth comb until I found Larry Christenson.

8

CRUSHED AGAIN

C ALLING INFORMATION, I was able to locate his church. With the number in hand, I picked up the receiver and started to dial. Something said, "Don't call—go." San Pedro wasn't far and I was at the explosion point anyway. So, I hopped in the car and, at low altitude, flew to San Pedro.

Arriving at the church, I was soon faced with another disappointment. Friday was his day off. "Oh no!" I said to myself, "not another dead-end street." His secretary told me that she thought he might be coming in for a special meeting—she wasn't positive, though.

I had come this far, so I decided to wait, hoping against hope that he would indeed come in. Leading me to a small prayer chapel, she said I could wait there and she would inform Pastor Christenson of my presence. I imagine she was wondering how I happened to be there. It was probably an unusual sight to see a black man come to a white Lutheran church to receive the gift of the Holy Spirit.

As I waited, I prayed and read. Oh, how I hoped that this was it! Presently, the door opened and Larry Christenson walked in, his face questioning. I related my experiences up to that moment, ending with my purpose for being there. He assured me that if I could wait until his meeting was over he would be most happy to talk with me.

I consented; after all, what else could I do? I was at the point of breaking open like a ripe watermelon. If I didn't get some help and guidance soon, as far as I was concerned, I was finished. I say finished, because I knew that I could not continue on in the ministry in the face of this emptiness and lack of *power.*

When he returned, we went into his office. After some time exchanging thoughts and relating my feelings and desires, he asked me if I was ready to receive the Holy Spirit. (Was I ready!) I indicated that I was.

When he suggested that we go into the sanctuary and kneel at the altar, I agreed. At this point, I was ready to stand on my head if necessary to receive the Holy Spirit. He gave me instructions—what to do, what to expect. What he said sounded exactly like what I had already done. The question arose, "It had not worked before, so how was it going to work now?"

He told me simply to ask the Lord Jesus to baptize me with the Holy Spirit and believe that He had done it. Then open my mouth, lift up the sound of my voice, and speak forth whatever words the Holy Spirit placed on my lips. I was tense with expectancy as I followed his instructions. All that came out of my mouth was the sound you hear when the doctor puts that awful tasting, little wooden stick in your mouth to hold your tongue down when he tells you to say *"aah."* You know the sound.

I could hear him praying in the most beautiful language. It was so fluent and rhythmical. Then he began to sing in this language. I tell you it was thrilling and so beautiful. He laid his hands on me and told me to *continue speaking.* I said to myself, "Speaking what? Is this supposed to be a language?" All that came out of my mouth was noise—like somebody choking. I thought, "If this is speaking in tongues, I surely wouldn't want anyone to hear me." To myself, I sounded like an idiot. I would be embarrassed for anyone to hear me making these silly noises.

Meanwhile, Pastor Christenson was saying to me, "That's right; that's right; you've got it; keep on speaking." I have to tell you the truth: it sounded ridiculous to me. Tears were streaming down my face; they were not tears of joy but tears of frustration and disappointment. I felt nothing but silly. Yet, Pastor Christenson encouraged me by assuring me that it was genuine. I was to keep right on speaking and the language would become, by use, more fluent and intelligible.

This is one objection I have with many of the books written today concerning the experience of people receiving the Holy Spirit. In most cases it seems that the most dramatic experiences are the only ones recorded. It leaves one with the expectation that everyone will experience this same beauty and fluency of tongues upon receiving the Holy Spirit. But as Pastor Christenson pointed out, and I have since found out myself after personally laying hands on and praying with many to receive the Holy Spirit, most do not get a full and fluent release at first.

Of course, this is no fault of the Holy Spirit because He is perfect and all His gifts and manifestations are equally perfect. But, we must always keep in mind that the manifestations must come through imperfect vessels. The knowledge that one possesses about what to expect and the all important aspect of yieldedness must be taken into account when evaluating a person's experience.

At this time, I thought that I was fully yielded. I was ready, but not fully yielded, as you shall see.

Pastor Christenson told me that mine was a legitimate experience and to continue praying in the Spirit, or speaking in tongues, as it is generally termed. Well, I wasn't fully convinced that anything had happened, other than the fact that I had sounded like an idiot. Remember, too, I felt nothing. I thought surely that something this important and spiritual should be, must be, attended by some very pronounced emotional feelings; and I was looking for them. But as the song so aptly puts it, it ain't necessarily so.

Driving back to Los Angeles, I was tormented with the thought, "If this is not a genuine experience, where do I go from here?" As I drove along, I tried to speak in this new tongue, but only that agonizingly ridiculous sound came out. It was night and dark outside, but it was even darker within me.

9

THE BEGINNING OF THE END

THE WEEK OF Monday, February 23, was a week of fear, frustration, and deep questionings. I told the Lord that if this was what it was all about—these ridiculous sounds—I would continue to speak out even though I sounded like an idiot. I certainly didn't want my wife and congregation to hear me, but I wanted the Holy Spirit; and if this was it, then I would just have to sound like a fool. I told the Lord that if I sounded foolish, it was all His fault because He never should have opened my heart and eyes to the gift of the Holy Spirit in the first place. As the week drew to a close, I thought surely I would experience some kind of feeling or emotion. You guessed it. Nothing.

My spiritual mother, Betty's Aunt Tena, had mentioned that the little Episcopal church that she had been attending was to have a revival meeting that week. It had completely slipped my mind in the midst of this spiritual search in which I had been engaged. I had almost lost contact with life itself. Jesus is marvelous in the way He works all things together for our good. Betty mentioned that she had talked to Tena and the revival was going well. I thought to myself, "I'm so tired, both physically and spiritually. I need to go somewhere and be ministered to." So I went. It was Friday night of the week of February 23, and it was to prove later to be the beginning of the end of my quest.

I arrived late and the service had already begun. They were singing hymns when I walked in and took my seat. They sang several more hymns; and indeed, it was refreshing after the week through which I had just come. There was a tall young man with a deep, rich, and powerful voice leading the singing. When the song service was over, he went into his own personal testimony concerning his Christian experience.

It was quite stirring, especially when he mentioned the fact that he was Jewish. He told about his conversion and some experiences surrounding it. Then he said something that almost rocked me off my pew. He related how empty and powerless his Christian life had been until he came face-to-face with the gift of the Holy Spirit.

At this point, I almost shouted with joy. I'm sure you can understand my enthusiasm. He told of how powerful and joyous his life was now because of his transforming encounter with the Holy Spirit. He told of the victory and peace he was experiencing in his every day Christian walk. My excitement was almost uncontrollable.

The thought occurred to me that this was the reason the Lord led me here tonight. I felt certain that this would be *my* night. One thing troubled me as he concluded his testimony. He never once mentioned speaking in other tongues.

I could hardly wait for the service to end so that I could ask him about the speaking in tongues as the sign and evidence of the infilling with the Holy Spirit. The main speaker for the revival was Dr. Robert Frost, author of *Aglow with the Spirit*.[1] (He plays a prominent role in this story as you shall see.)

At the conclusion of the service, I made a straight course for this young Jewish fellow. After talking to him for a few minutes, I broached this question of speaking with other tongues. He immediately and joyously exclaimed his own glorious experience with this manifestation and of the joy and power in prayer and boldness that accompanied it. I was thrilled at hearing this and began relating my own experience— and failure, or so I thought—in receiving the Holy Spirit. As we talked, another young man who had given his testimony that night and Dr. Frost moved close and joined us.

Everyone was moving into the fellowship hall, directly behind the main sanctuary, for refreshments and fellowship. As I continued speaking, Dr. Frost chimed in with the joyous statement that he was sure that I had indeed received the Holy Spirit. I say joyous statement because he had an expression on his face like one who had just found hidden treasure. He informed me that all I needed was what he termed "a full release."

He suggested that the four of us go into the sanctuary for prayer. He further suggested that the three of them lay hands on me while we prayed for this release. I knelt at the altar and they surrounded me. Dr. Frost told me to just open my mouth and speak forth the words that the Holy Spirit placed on my tongue. In my heart I was saying, "Oh no! Not that again." As they laid hands on me and began praying in unknown tongues, I was thrilled. It sounded so beautiful.

Picture this if you will: three men praying in three different unknown languages at the same time. You would naturally tend to think this would be utter confusion. But believe me when I tell you, it sounded like water cascading over a waterfall. It was beautiful, joyous, and thrilling. I felt as though I were in the very presence of God Himself.

Well, I opened my mouth as instructed, and guess what came out? That's right! That same ridiculous sound that ushered forth when Larry Christenson prayed for me. The most amazing thing to me was to hear the three of them saying to me, "That's right; you've got it; it's coming; keep it up; praise God it's coming through!"

This was a nightmare. Here I was, in all sincerity, trying my best to receive something real and genuine and all that came forth were these ridiculous sounds. Tears were streaming down my face as I, with great intensity and determination, was trying to pray in these unknown tongues. I was completely crushed at this point. When I arose from my knees, they embraced me and with joy on their faces they praised the Lord that I had come through.

We went back to the fellowship hall and everyone was thrilled because I had come through. Aunt Tena was there and she was full of love and joy. Everyone was having a ball.

Meantime, I was torn up inside; I felt like a hypocrite. Honestly, I had felt nothing. I smiled weakly and tried to play the part of the conquering hero, but inside I was in a state of utter frustration.

On the way home, I questioned within myself, wondering what was happening to me. These people had been sincere; I couldn't deny that. And yet, I felt empty and unfulfilled.

10

THE CROWNING DAY: THE RIVER BEGINS TO FLOW

Saturday, February 28, 1970, was to be an unforgettable day in my life, a day that would foreshadow a complete revolution in my ministry. Praise be to God! I slept late Saturday morning and actually had to force myself out of bed. I felt terrible, frustrated, discouraged. I went to the barbershop late that afternoon for my regular haircut. As I was leaving, the thought came to me to go over to Tena's. She had only encouraging words for me. She told me about the wonderful service they'd had that afternoon and suggested that the two of us go together to the final service that night. I didn't feel much like doing anything, but I consented.

The service that night was held in the fellowship hall. There were about thirty of us there, sitting in a semicircle. We must have sung about twenty-five or thirty songs; and it was surely a blessing to me, especially the way that I was feeling then.

Finally, Dr. Frost rose to give his closing message. He announced that the Lord had laid it upon his heart to talk about his own experience with the Holy Spirit, at least some facets of it. He said that quite frankly he'd had a problem with "feelings." He related how the Lord took him step-by-step and revealed to him that it wasn't by feelings that we receive the Holy Spirit but by faith and faith alone. A beautiful bright light went on inside of me.

As he talked, the Lord revealed to me that there is only one way to receive anything from God and that is by faith in what God has promised in His Word. Praise God! Praise God! Praise God! Now I knew. My problem was that I wanted to feel something before I would be willing to accept what God, very plainly, says in His Word is received by faith and faith alone. The dark clouds began to roll back and the sky became as clear as crystal. This was it! I had indeed received the gift of the Holy Spirit the very first time I prayed and asked the Lord to baptize me, after reading those first books.

My problem was that I wouldn't accept God's gift on God's terms. I had my own mind made up as to how it would happen, and because of that I had missed the joy and blessing. Well, it would appear that all was well now; but alas, there was one more river to cross. And praise His wonderful name, the Lord was present to cross it with me.

At the conclusion of the service, Dr. Frost inquired if there were any that needed ministering to. Something on the inside of me said, "Have them pray for you." That was the Holy Spirit. Immediately, Satan spoke up, and these thoughts crossed my mind: "I can't have anyone pray for me after last night. I would be repudiating everything that happened last night. And, too, I am a minister of the gospel and I should be praying for others instead of them praying for me." No one responded to the offer of ministry, so Dr. Frost turned the service over to the minister of the church. Again, he asked if anyone needed to be ministered to. Again the voice on the inside said, "Have them pray for you." Again Satan spoke up: "You'll look like a fool asking them to pray for you. What kind of minister will they think you are?" By now we had joined hands and formed a circle to dismiss.

The minister was praying the closing prayer. Desperation rose up within me. I knew that this was it. It's now or never. As the amen was spoken and we had just loosed our hands, I fell to my knees in the center of the circle. I poured out my heart with tears. I told of my conflict over feelings, my misery, my desire to be free.

The group moved in and I felt many hands on my

head and many voices raised in prayer on my behalf. I opened my mouth and began to speak, and that mighty river began to flow. Torrents of unknown words poured out of my mouth. In faith I had spoken and the Holy Spirit gave me the utterance—just as He had given nineteen hundred years ago on the day of Pentecost.

It's real, my friends, it's real! Praise God, it's real! I could hardly believe it. Here I was, speaking in unknown tongues just as Peter, James, and John had done so many centuries before. I was thrilled. I was filled with peace and joy and a dynamic sense of power—the power of God Himself. I had at last entered the realm of the Spirit. From this glorious day forward I would *walk by faith and not by sight* (1 Cor. 5:7).

11

JOY UNSPEAKABLE AND FULL OF GLORY

MUCH TIME HAS come and gone since that crossing of the Jordan into the Promised Land, February 28, 1970. My whole life has changed. My ministry has been anointed by the Spirit. The joy and victory in prayer is unsurpassed. I'm still on cloud one hundred and climbing. Can you believe that? Praise God!

Our congregation has been transformed. The consecration and dedication of many since they have received the fullness of the Spirit has been a joy to behold. The spiritual fiber and enthusiasm of the body of believers are at a fervent peak. Their outreach into the community has been spectacular.

On November 26, 1973, we moved into a new facility—Crenshaw Christian Center. In July of 1977, because of the vast increase in the number of people coming to the Center, we had to go to three Sunday

39

morning worship services. At two of the services we were regularly putting about 1,300 people in our auditorium plus several hundred people in our gym building where we had closed-circuit television. In the three services we were ministering to more than 3,000 people per Sunday. Praise God! Our membership was more than 2,600. (Our membership would eventually grow to more than 20,000.)

Our worship services were tremendous! We taught the Word. On a regular basis, as part of the service as the Lord directed, we had the vocal ministry gifts in operation—prophecy and divers kinds of tongues with interpretation of tongues. People were healed while they were sitting in the audience. We saw miracles.

We actually had people standing in line—arriving an hour early to stand in line so that they could get in. Of course, it's the Lord that sends the people. We preach the Word; He sends the people.

12

DEAR READER

MAY I SAY to you, dear reader, that if there is a longing for a deeper and closer walk with the Lord, a desire to really see the power of God manifested in these times and to experience that perfect joy and peace, may I point you to Him who baptizes with the Holy Spirit. You, too, can receive the power that makes it possible to pray without ceasing, to overcome every temptation, and to cast off every vile and wicked habit that you have striven with tears to shed with no success. Believe me, you need the power of the Holy Spirit manifested in your everyday walk so you can live the victorious life.

Cast aside your doubts and all your preconceived ideas about the gift of the Holy Spirit and the speaking with other tongues. Satan has very cleverly blinded many in regard to these great issues. Many have rejected the blessings that God desires to pour out upon all His children because some noted theologian declared that these manifestations only happened in the early church; that we don't need signs and miracles and the manifestation of the power and might of the Spirit of God today.

Surely, if for a moment you look around, the evidence is overwhelming—we need something. Look in the churches—we need something. *We need the power of the Holy Spirit.*

You may need something in your own personal Christian life. If you have not yet experienced the enabling power of the Holy Spirit, receive Him today. Jesus is waiting and eager to immerse you in the Holy Spirit, that the rivers of living water that John tells us about in the Gospel (John 7:38–39) may begin to flow out of your life. Jesus is waiting. Don't be led astray by anyone. Search the scriptures. What I have told you is truth. And the truth will set you free (John 8:32).

Our authority is the Word of God (2 Tim. 3:16–17). Read God's Word with a heart ready to receive His revealed truth concerning the baptism with the Holy Spirit and speaking with other tongues. May I further suggest that you specifically read the Book of Acts and 1 Corinthians, chapters 12, 13, 14. I know that the Lord will reveal Himself and His truth to you in this most important matter, as He has to me.

The following are some tips that will help you to receive the gift of the Holy Spirit when you are ready:

∞ POINT 1

The first point which is absolutely essential as you prepare to receive the gift of the Holy Spirit is that you must have accepted Jesus Christ as your personal Lord and Savior. John 7:38–39 informs us that the promise of the Holy Spirit is made only to believers. By no means should anyone who is not a believer pray for the gift of the Holy Spirit! However, if you are a believer and are assured of your salvation, then you are ready and should enter into this deeper spiritual dimension. The following are some scriptures you may check to be sure of your salvation:

John 1:12

John 3:3, 5

John 3:16, 18, 36

John 5:24

John 6:47

John 20:31

Acts 16:31

Ephesians 2:8-9

If you have checked these scriptures and say, "I don't know if that's me or not; I'm not sure," or "No, I know that's not me. I've never received Jesus," it can be you and you can be sure. Today is the day of salvation (2 Cor. 6:2). Read Romans 10:9–10, which says:

> That if thou shalt confess with thy mouth the Lord Jesus, and shalt believe in thine heart that God hath raised him from the dead, thou shalt be saved. For with the heart man believeth unto righteousness; and with the mouth confession is made unto salvation.

Do you believe that God raised Jesus Christ from the dead? Will you confess Jesus as the Lord of your life? If you answer yes to these two questions, then pray the following simple prayer and become a member of the family of God:

> *Jesus, I need to be born again. I need a Savior; I need You. I turn from sin and turn to You. I believe in my heart that God raised You from the dead, and I ask You now to come into my heart and be the Lord of my life. I receive You now as Lord of my life and I confess with my mouth that Jesus is my Lord. Thank You, Jesus.*

Romans 10:13 says that "whosoever shall call upon the name of the Lord shall be saved." You have called upon the name of the Lord; salvation is yours NOW. The scriptures listed under Point 1 now apply to you. Confess them as yours.

You are now ready for Point 2.

∽ POINT 2

Keep in mind that the Bible teaches us that the Holy Spirit is given freely by grace to help and enable us to move into the deeper areas of our Christian experience and to achieve victory in our daily witness for Christ. Remember, too, that this gift of the Holy Spirit is not given as an attainment or reward based on some supposed degree of holiness, but based alone on the fact that Jesus promised to give Him to every believer. Following are some scriptures you may want to check:

John 7:38–39

John 14:16–17

John 14:25–26

John 15:16

John 16:7

John 16:12-14

∞ POINT 3

When receiving the gift of the Holy Spirit, it helps to be with a group of Spirit-filled Christians who can instruct, encourage, and pray with you. Although it is not essential, I personally find it to be a great help for two specific reasons.

First, because it is scriptural: Acts 8:17, 9:17, and 19:6 show us how others may help us by the laying on of hands as a point of faith release.

Second, because Satan will immediately challenge the believer as to the authenticity of his experience. It's good to have the witness of Christians who can affirm the authenticity of the experience.

∞ POINT 4

If one is a sincere seeker after the truth concerning receiving the gift of the Holy Spirit and has read all the scriptures suggested, he will see beyond any doubt that the baptism with the Holy Spirit is meant for every believer today. Suggested reading:

The Book of Acts

1 Corinthians, chapters 12, 13, 14

Joel 2:28–29

Matthew 3:11

Luke 3:16

Mark 1:8

John 14:16–17

John 1:33

Mark 16:17

Luke 11:9–13

Luke 24:49

John 7:38–39

John 15:16

John 16:7, 12–14

Acts 1:4–8

Acts 2:4, 38–39

John 14:25–26

∞ POINT 5

Now that you are ready to receive, simply pray the prayer of invitation—inviting Jesus, the Baptizer with the Holy Spirit, to baptize you with the Spirit. Suggested prayer:

> *Father, I believe with all my heart, based on the scriptures, that the gift of the Holy Spirit is meant for me. Just as I trust You for my eternal salvation by faith, so now*

> *do I trust You, by faith, to give me the*
> *fullness of the Holy Spirit with the evi-*
> *dence of speaking with other tongues. I*
> *now receive, by faith, the gift of the Holy*
> *Spirit within. Thank You, in Jesus' name,*
> *amen.*

∞ POINT 6

Now release the Spirit by praising the Lord in unknown tongues, by faith, as the Spirit gives the utterance or language. Remember the Holy Spirit doesn't do the speaking; you do. This is what happened to the disciples on the day of Pentecost. Why should the Lord deal any differently with you? He is no respecter of persons or denominations. By faith, open your mouth and yield your tongue to the Holy Spirit. Trust Him to give you a language of praise. Initiate syllables with your tongue and lips. Remember that even when you attempt to speak in your own familiar language, unless you open your mouth, give the sound of your voice, and move your tongue and lips, nothing comes out, does it? Often unfamiliar words will flash into your mind. Speak them out in praise to the Lord. The more yielded and believing you become, the more fluent and free the language will become.

If at first your language doesn't "flow," don't become discouraged or doubt that you received the gift of the Holy Spirit. The devil may suggest to you that you are making it all up; don't listen to him. Remember, he is a liar and the father of lies (John 8:44).

Be obedient to the Lord and keep praying and singing in the spirit. Continue to praise God for filling you as He promised. Continue stepping out in faith by yielding your voice to the Lord. He will surely give you the fulfillment of the desire of your heart. If at all possible, seek other Spirit-filled believers with whom you can fellowship and pray in the Spirit. Continue to exercise your gift daily.

If you would claim your rightful New Testament inheritance in Christ, begin by receiving the Holy Spirit with the evidence of speaking in other tongues. Remember, this is not an end, it is just the beginning; it ushers you through a spiritual doorway into the supernatural realm of spiritual blessing.

Potentially you have become a powerful and effective witness for Jesus Christ, so don't let the devil rob you of God's best. Keep your eyes on Jesus, "the author and finisher of our faith" (Heb. 12:2); hold fast to the Word of God which abides forever and soon you will be firmly grounded in this new life in the Spirit.

Thanks be to God for his inexpressible gift!
—2 CORINTHIANS 9:15, ESV

NOTES

1
THE MISSING LINK

1. Kathryn Kuhlman, *I Believe in Miracles* (Englewood Cliffs, N.J.: Prentice-Hall, 1964)

2
SEEK AND YE SHALL FIND

1. Kathryn Kuhlman, *God Can Do It Again* (Englewood Cliffs, N.J.: Prentice-Hall, 1969).

5
A FRIEND SPEAKS

1. Don Basham, *Face Up with a Miracle* (Northridge, Calif.: Voice Christian Publications, 1969).
2. John Sherrill, *They Speak with Other Tongues* (New York: McGraw-Hill, 1965).
3. John H. Osteen, *This Awakening Generation* (Humble, Tex.: Osteen Publications, 1970).

6
LIGHT AND DARKNESS

1. Basham.

9
THE BEGINNING OF THE END

1. Robert C. Frost, *Aglow with the Spirit* (Northridge, Calif.: Voice Christian Publications, 1965).

ABOUT THE AUTHOR

APOSTLE FREDERICK K.C. Price is the founder of Crenshaw Christian Center (CCC) in Los Angeles, California. He began CCC in 1973, and shepherded it through 35 years into a ministry of world renown, with services held since 1989 in the 10,000-seat FaithDome.

In 1978, Apostle Price received instruction from God to begin a television broadcast. As a result, *Ever Increasing Faith Ministries* (EIFM) was launched, appearing initially in five of the nation's big-city television markets. Since that time, the broadcast has become global, and EIFM can be viewed on 132 stations in all fifty states and in six foreign countries. The broadcast is also heard on fifteen radio programs and nineteen Internet broadcast stations, including the *Ever Increasing Faith* website. Additionally, it can be seen on YouTube, Vimeo, and Christian.tv.

In 1990, Apostle Price founded the Fellowship of Inner-City Word of Faith Ministries (FICWFM), now renamed the Fellowship of International Christian Word of Faith Ministries. And in 2001, he established an East Coast church—Crenshaw Christian Center East.

A visionary and widely respected teacher, he is the author of some fifty books on faith, healing, prosperity, the Holy Spirit, and other subjects. His book *How Faith Works* is a recognized classic on the operation of faith and its life-changing principles. He has also authored three historic volumes under the title of *Race, Religion & Racism*. Apostle Price has sold nearly three million books since 1976. His most recent works include: *The Mind: The Arena of Faith*, *Prosperity: Good News for God's People*, and *Answered Prayer Guaranteed: The Power of Praying with Faith.*

Although Apostle Price had already begun operating under the mantle of apostle, in 2008 he was publicly affirmed as an apostle of faith. Under his gift as teacher, he established several schools for ministry and formal education on the grounds of CCC. Among them are Frederick K.C. Price III Christian Schools (preschool to 12th grade) and the Apostle Price Ministry Training Institute. Over the years, Apostle Price has received many prestigious awards—most notably, the Horatio Alger Award from the Horatio Alger Association of Distinguished Americans and the Southern Christian Leadership Council's Kelly Miller Smith Interfaith Award, both in 1998.

Apostle Price holds an honorary doctorate of divinity from Oral Roberts University in Tulsa, Oklahoma, and an honorary diploma from Rhema Bible Training Center in Broken Arrow, Oklahoma.

A year after his affirmation as apostle, and after more than thirty-five years as pastor, Apostle Price stepped aside to formally install his son, Frederick K. Price Jr., as pastor. He is currently the presiding prelate of CCC West and East, and serves at the helm as the chairman of CCC's board of directors. Apostle Price not only ministers in the FaithDome, but travels extensively, mostly in the United States, teaching the uncompromising Word of God.

A devoted husband, Apostle Price has been married to Dr. Betty R. Price for more than sixty years. They are the proud parents of four children, and have ten grandchildren, and four great-grandchildren.

OTHER BOOKS BY
THE AUTHOR

How Faith Works

Race, Religion & Racism, Volume 1: A Bold Encounter with Division in the Church

Race, Religion & Racism, Volume 2: Perverting the Gospel to Subjugate a People

Race, Religion & Racism, Volume 3: Jesus, Christianity and Islam

How to Obtain Strong Faith: Six Principles

The Holy Spirit: The Helper We All Need

The Mind: The Arena of Faith

Integrity: The Guarantee for Success

Prosperity: Good News for God's People

Living in Hostile Territory: A Survival Guide for the Overcoming Christian

Answered Prayer Guaranteed: The Power of Praying with Faith

Faith, Foolishness, or Presumption?

Identified with Christ: A Complete Cycle from Defeat to Victory

The Christian Family: Practical Insight for Family Living

Dr. Price's Golden Nuggets: A Treasury of Wisdom for Both Ministers and Laypeople

Five Little Foxes of Faith

The Chastening of the Lord

Testing the Spirits

Beware! The Lies of Satan

The Way, the Walk, and the Warfare of the Believer: A Verse-by-Verse Study of the Book of Ephesians

Three Keys to Positive Confession

The Promised Land: A New Era for the Body of Christ

A New Law for a New People

The Victorious, Overcoming Life: A Verse-by-Verse Study of the Book of Colossians

Practical Suggestions for Successful Ministry

Living in the Realm of the Spirit

The Holy Spirit: The Missing Ingredient

Is Healing for All?

MINIBOOKS

The Truth About Death

The Truth About Disasters

The Truth About Fate

The Truth About Fear

The Truth About Homosexuality

The Truth About Race

The Truth About Worry

The Truth About Giving

Now Faith Is

How to Believe God for a Mate

Thank God for Everything?

Concerning Those Who Have Fallen Asleep

The Origin of Satan

SPECIALTY-SIZE BOOKS

Walking in God's Word: Through His Promises

Words of Wisdom: Wow!

Building on a Firm Foundation

Homosexuality: State of Birth or State of Mind?

SPANISH LANGUAGE BOOKS

Como Creer en Dios para Encontrar tu Pareja

Edificandonos Sobre Una Base Firme: Una Guia para el Desarrollo de Su Cristiana

CONTACT THE AUTHOR

For more information on books by Apostle Frederick K.C. Price or to be placed on the *Ever Increasing Faith* mailing list,

Call:

    (800) 927-3436

Or write:

    Crenshaw Christian Center
    P.O. Box 90000
    Los Angeles, CA 90009

Or check your local TV or Webcast listing:

    Ever Increasing Faith Ministries

Visit our website at:

    www.faithdome.org

NOTES

NOTES

NOTES

NOTES

NOTES

NOTES

_____

_____

_____

_____

_____

_____

_____

_____

_____

_____

_____

_____

_____

_____

NOTES